FEAST
of the
BEAST

FEAST
OF THE
BEAST

TEXE MARRS

ACKNOWLEDGEMENTS

My staff deserves maximum praise for their outstanding contributions. Included: Michelle Powell, business administrator, Sandra Myers, publishing and art; Jerry Barrett, computer and internet; Nelson Sorto, shipping and facilities manager; and Steve Reilly, administration and shipping. To my wife and confidant, Wanda Marrs, goes all my love and gratefulness.

Feast of the Beast

Cover design: Texe Marrs and Sandra Myers

Printed in the United States of America

Library of Congress Catalog Card Number 2016963764

Categories: 1. Religion 2. Bible Prophecy 3. Christianity 4. Judaism

ISBN 978-1-930004-02-3

Fire Came Down From God

"And they went up on the breadth of the earth, and compassed the camp of the saints about, and the beloved city: and fire came down from God out of heaven, and devoured them."

—*Revelation 20:9*

OTHER BOOKS BY RIVERCREST PUBLISHING

The Destroyer, by Texe Marrs

Holy Serpent of the Jews, by Texe Marrs

Pastors and Churches Gone Wild, by Texe Marrs

DNA Science and the Jewish Bloodline, by Texe Marrs

Conspiracy of the Six-Pointed Star, by Texe Marrs

Conspiracy World, by Texe Marrs

Mysterious Monuments: Encyclopedia of Secret Illuminati Designs, Masonic Architecture, and Occult Places, by Texe Marrs

Codex Magica: Secret Signs, Mysterious Symbols and Hidden Codes of the Illuminati, by Texe Marrs

Matrix of Gog: From the Land of Magog Came the Khazars to Destroy and Plunder, by Daniel Patrick

Synagogue of Satan: The Secret History of Jewish World Domination, by Andrew Carrington Hitchcock

Protocols of the Learned Elders of Zion

Days of Hunger, Days of Chaos, by Texe Marrs

Project L.U.C.I.D.: The Beast 666 Universal Human Control System, by Texe Marrs

Circle of Intrigue: The Hidden Inner Circle of the Global Illuminati Conspiracy, by Texe Marrs

Dark Majesty: The Secret Brotherhood and the Magic of a Thousand Points of Light, by Texe Marrs

New Age Cults and Religions, by Texe Marrs

Mystery Mark of the New Age, by Texe Marrs

Dark Secrets of the New Age, by Texe Marrs

TABLE OF Contents

INTRODUCTION

Digging in the Wall

In *Ezekiel 8*, the Prophet describes the vision given him by God of the secret heresies of the elders of the House of Israel. Lifted up from earth, he was brought in the visions of God to Jerusalem and to the gate of the altar of the sanctuary. "Son of man," said God, "seest thou what they do? Even the great abominations that the house of Israel committeth here…"

"And he brought me to the door of the court;" writes the prophet, "and when I looked, behold a hole in the wall. Then He said unto me, Son of man, dig now in the wall: and when I had digged in the wall, behold a door."

"And He said unto me, Go in, and behold the wicked abominations that they do here."

"So I went in and saw, and behold every form of creeping things, and abominable beasts, and all the idols of the House of Israel, portrayed upon the wall round about."

Thus was Ezekiel commanded by God to dig in the wall, to behold a door and secret chambers. There he saw unimaginable dark creatures and creeping things painted on the walls. The seventy men of the ancients of the house of Israel were there, with incense, and they were worshipping those abominable creatures. And Ezekiel was told by God that not only did the ancients of the house of Israel worship these abominations but that they had filled the land with violence and provoked God's anger.

The terrible consequences of this secret worship by thc Elders of Zion, "every man in the chambers of his imagery," were spelled out by God. We read, in *Ezekiel 9:3* that, "The glory of the God of Israel was gone…"

Likewise, today, in this, the 21st century of our Lord and Saviour, I ask you, dear friends, to do as Ezekiel was told to do in the book of Ezekiel. Yes, by all means, dig in the wall and see what is happening today in the house of Israel. Unbeknownst to the world, even in the face of ignorant Christians who would make excuses for their ungodly behavior, you will discover a hole. Look in and see. The rabbinical elders of Israel today are indeed worshipping creeping things abominable to God. *Even the Beast of Revelation 9 and 11, Leviathan, the crooked and piercing serpent, is portrayed in the chambers of their imagery.*

Yes, the Jews—in their unholy religion, Judaism—secretly but fervently worship Leviathan, the serpent, to whom they pray and entreat. This vain worship is reflected moreover in the most holy books of the Jews; that is, in their Kabbalah and in their Babylonian Talmud. Yet, the Christian Church and its leadership knows little or nothing of this strange and wicked worship. To these Christian leaders, the Jewish religion is both holy and pious; it lacks, of course, the Messiah, Jesus. But as a religion, it is viewed as sufficient.

The ignorance of Christian leadership in the matter of the abominations practiced by the rabbis is monumental and is gravely injurious both to the Jews and to Christian believers.

This book, ***Feast of the Beast***, will hopefully remedy some of this ignorance. My prayer as author is that at least some Jews will read these pages and come to realize the horror of their satanic religion. In so doing, may they go on to study the life and truth of Jesus Christ. Only He will prove to be sufficient for their needs.

I also am very hopeful that Judaizer Christians, in reading this book, will understand that Judaism is a dreadful religion offering no hope for the Jews. May the Christian return fully to Jesus Christ and cherish the New Covenant which leads to happiness and to eternal salvation.

—Texe Marrs
Austin, Texas

ONE

My Discovery of the Abominations of Judaism

In the 1980s I was urged by the Holy Spirit to research the New Age movement, an occult revival very much in evidence at the time, and to write about it from a Christian perspective. This research resulted in my authoring about a dozen books over several years, including *Dark Secrets of the New Age* and *New Age Cults and Religions*.

In my research for these books, I continually came upon mention of Jewish subjects which originated in the *Kabbalah* or the *Babylonian Talmud*. The Kabbalah, for example, was a staple offering at the many New Age and occult bookstores which I frequented, and the Talmud was often favorably referred to by many bestselling New Age authors in their books.

The Kabbalah: Primary Source of Global Evil

I soon found that the doctrines and teachings of most of the religions of the New Age movement were right out of the pages of the Kabbalah. The *Kabbalah* is the source of virtually all the world's false religions and other religious groups. Whether that group is Freemasonry, or Wicca, or even the various UFO societies or an Illuminati secret order, its basic formulation and teachings are from the Kabbalah.

How could the books of Kabbalah, written and compiled by ancient Jewish rabbis, be the basis for so much evil and wickedness? The devilish origins of Kabbalah are phenomenal in their ability to deceive and to darken minds.

The Babylonian Talmud: Traditions of Men

Next, I investigated the *Babylonian Talmud*, which is the books containing the 613 laws of Judaism and the commentary to support these laws. The Talmud's official name is the *Babylonian Talmud* because the writings of ancient rabbis came out of Israel's Babylonian captivity during the days of Jeremiah, Daniel, and Nehemiah. During Jesus' era, these laws and commentary were oral, but in 300 to 400 AD, the chief rabbis committed them to writing. Jesus testified as to the "hypocrisy" of the Talmudic doctrines and stated that they are not of God but are the "traditions of men."

The Babylonian Talmud is called by Supreme Court Justice Ruth Bader Ginsburg her "guide for daily living." Many Jews insist the Talmud is so much greater than the Bible. It empowers the rabbis, we are told, and inflates the sense of self-worth of the Jews. Here are just a few actual comments by rabbis regarding their Talmud.

> "God must submit to the decisions of a majority vote of the rabbis."
>
> —Rabbi Metzger

> "The Babylonian Talmud represents god in

the flesh."

—Rabbi Neusner

"Only insignificant people study the Bible."

—Rabbi Gradzinski

"A rabbi decrees, and God obeys."

—Rabbi Eliakh

"Talmud study leads to saintliness and purity while Bible study does not even produce righteousness."

—Rabbi Mandelbaum

"Even the Almighty studies the Talmud."

—Rabbi Mandelbaum

Gauging from these comments by top rabbis, the Talmud is utterly blasphemous. Yet, it is the doctrinal font for modern-day Judaism.

Talmud and Kabbalah are Interconnected

I have discovered that much of the Talmud is actually based on the Kabbalah. One cannot separate the two if an understanding of the Judaic religion is to be understood.

Christian pastors and laymen, including top theologians and Bible teachers, do not study the Kabbalah and Talmud. They erroneously assume that Judaism is based strictly on the Old Testament. This is not so. In fact, Jewish Yeshivas (religious schools or seminaries) almost exclusively study the Talmud and Kabbalah. Rarely is the Torah (the first five books of the Old Testament) even referred to.

Most rabbis believe the Old Testament's actual words to

be based on mythologies. They study the Talmud and advise their laypersons based on its advice and commentary or perhaps they study the Torah using gematria (numbers) and kabbalistic methodologies. More advanced rabbis assiduously study the works of only the Kabbalah.

Grievous mistakes and miscalculations result from the ignorance of Christians who believe that Judaism is based solely on the Old Testament. The truth is that Jesus Himself told us that the Jews believed not the commandments of God but, instead, trusted in the *"traditions of the elders"* which effectively nullified the Word of God. The "traditions of the elders" are what we find in the Kabbalah and Talmud, as opposed to the truths in the books of the Old and New Testament.

Feast of the Beast

When I figuratively dug in the wall and looked therein, I realized that just as was discovered by the prophet Ezekiel so long ago, the Jews are once again betraying God. Today's rabbis have brought to the average Jews the worship of "wicked abominations"—creeping things, and abominable beasts.

Amazingly, the Judaic religion now portrays the beast that rises out of the bottomless pit *(Revelation 9)* as their life-long companion, friend, and protector. They say this is *Leviathan*, whom they describe as a huge, fish-like serpent. To the Jews, *Leviathan*, is in fact, the *Holy Serpent.*

Someday, perhaps very soon, Leviathan will rise. He will emerge from the watery abyss to lead the Jewish people in their eschatological victory over the Gentiles. It is Leviathan that will possess the Jews. They believe that Leviathan will produce divinity in their collective flesh. All this will manifest, say the Jews in their Kabbalah and Talmud, on the

Day of Purification. On that day, they will celebrate their great victory. They will become the very *"People of the Serpent."* They will cherish the Light of Leviathan as they consume his body in a great *Feast of the Beast*.

You are now invited to understand and to view in advance this great Feast of the Beast.

TWO

That Day When the Serpent King and His People Shall Rule

The New Era of Leviathan

"He (Leviathan the Serpent) beholdeth all high things: he is a king over all the children of pride."

—*Job 41:34*

"The Leviathan is thus a universal symbol of the new era in which the righteous (the Jews and their faithful servants among the Gentiles) will prosper and the wicked suffer… It is an ideal symbol of a new economic order in the world."

—Rabbi Michael Higger
The Jewish Utopia

The rabbinical sages who embrace the Kabbalah and Talmud worship a strange god whose shocking identity they conceal. While publicly they claim allegiance and fidelity to "Yah" (Yahweh) or Jehovah, their holy and sacred books of Kabbalah teach that the real name of God has been lost. The very nature of this god, they say, is ineffable, mysterious, unable to directly communicate, and unknown.

But amazingly, we discover that this Judaic deity is described in some detail, though in symbolic and allegorical language and terminology. Using these occult means, we come to the mind-boggling reality that the true God of the Jews is none other than the Serpent. In fact, he is the "piercing Serpent" whose name is Leviathan.

The Age of Leviathan

The Age of Leviathan is almost upon us. It is to be a "new era" of prosperity for the Jews. So complete will be the rule of the Jews over the nations of the world and the *goyim* (Gentiles) that they and their King shall be recognized and honored as the "Light of the World." Moreover, the "emblem" of Judaism shall be Leviathan the Serpent, and this emblem, or sign, shall dominate the world.

In the Old Testament book of *Job*, we are introduced to the Judaic Serpent. He is named *"Leviathan, the piercing serpent."* Leviathan is a symbolic representation of Satan, the Devil, whom the New Testament's book of *Revelation* identifies as "that old serpent, Satan, the dragon." Satan is, of course, yet another name for Lucifer, the serpent who seduced Eve in the Garden of Eden.

Now any student of the scriptures, including the ones schooled in the Jewish religion, well knows that Leviathan is Satan and is the Adversary of the one true God in heaven.

An ancient painting depicting Leviathan, the beast/fish encircling a red earth. Red, or scarlet, is the color of the harlot in *Revelation 17.*

That fact makes quite remarkable the adoption by the rabbis of this symbol and, indeed, of the title "Leviathan" as representative of the Jewish People and their quest for global power and a Zionist kingdom. Clearly, the satanic Jews are bold and audacious in their unseemly, yet highly revealing choice of symbols and names.

If a person ever for a moment doubted that Jesus was accurate and fairly told the truth when he bluntly told the Jews, *"Ye are of your father the devil,"* that doubt can certainly be erased. The Jews themselves declare their evil by bragging, in effect, *"We are the People of the Serpent of Leviathan, and with Satan's power on our side, we shall conquer the world!"*

Serpent to Reign Over Jewish Utopia

As if to emphasize their sinister and prideful confession of evil, in *The Jewish Utopia*, highly regarded Rabbi Michael Higger, Ph.D., boasts that Leviathan, the serpent who on the Jews behalf, shall pierce the world, will be for the Jews a fabulous, fulfilling gourmet meal. Yes, the whole world shall be on the menu and be consumed. Higger writes:

> "The Lord, finally, will prepare a feast for the upright. He has salted the huge Leviathan and has prepared the best food, fruit, fish, and meat for that purpose. The feast will be limitless."

This is the satanic counterfeit of the banquet, or feast, prepared in Heaven for the Bride of Christ.

Painting a bizarre—in my view, horrific and frightening—image of the future to come when the Jewish Utopia, world conquest, is realized, Higger quotes R. Johann, another rabbinical authority, in saying that in the correctly understood meaning of the tradition of Leviathan, "The Lord will in the future make a hut (home) for the righteous out of a part of the skin of the Leviathan." And the skin of the great snake, said Johann, will be placed on the walls of Jerusalem and shall serve as a *light*.

Symbolically this means that by taking on the manifestation of being the Serpent People, the Jews will be the *light of the world*. They will be a Holy People to be adored and emulated:

> "...and its light will shine forth from one end of the world to the other, as it says, And nations shall walk at thy light, and Kings at the brightness of thy rising."

Leviathan the Serpent Will Enlighten the World

What a shocking revelation: Leviathan is the Jewish People, and the light they shine to the world is the light of Lucifer, worshipped by occultists and Satanists the world over as "Father of Light" and honored by Alice Bailey's Lucis Trust as the "Solar Logos." Paul, in the New Testament, wisely warned that Satan the deceiver comes forth disguised as the "Angel of Light." Now we find that the god of Talmudic Judaism is none other than this same Father of Light, whose very skin (covering), affixed on the walls of Jerusalem, will enlighten the world. Yes, Judaism's Lucifer comes as the "Light of the World."

Any doubts in this regard are swept away by Dr. Higger's follow-up comments in *The Jewish Utopia*, in which he makes this remarkable statement:

> "The Leviathan is thus a universal symbol of the new era in which the righteous will prosper and the wicked suffer. The Leviathan, furthermore, is the emblem of the ideal age, when this world will become the home of the righteous. It is an ideal symbol of a new economic order in the world, when righteousness will be one's only requisite for acceptance into the realm of happiness and prosperity."

An artist's depiction of Leviathan devouring human victims. Since in Judaism he is helpmate and positive guide for Jews, the victims here are Gentiles, whom the Jews teach will be destroyed on the Day of Purification leading up to the Feast of Leviathan.

You will recall that this same Rabbi Michael Higger defines the *"righteous"* as all Jews plus the Gentiles who renounce their idolatrous, formerly believed-in faiths—such as Christianity—and agree to serve the Jews' god and become slaves to the Jewish masters. Only the "righteous" will be allowed to live. The other Gentiles are the "wicked" and will be exterminated. If you wish to partake of the Jews' "new civilization" (Higger, *The Jewish Utopia*, p. 18), you must worship Leviathan.

Global citizens, meet your future god—Leviathan, the piercing serpent, redeemer, and savior of the regal Jews, Kings of Zion, Light of the World!

"Do Not Make a Covenant with Leviathan"

What does God have to say about the Jews' covenant with Leviathan? Having seen how, in the envisioned Jewish Utopia, Leviathan represents the cabalistic rabbis' ideal and their ensign and symbol of their "new economic order," we next turn to God's Word in the book of *Job*, where we astonishingly discover that God examines and unmasks this very same Leviathan. Let us see what His counsel and judgement are concerning the Serpent god of Zion.

In the Scriptures regarding this great serpent, Leviathan, God counsels Job, his suffering servant, to withstand Leviathan and to not make a "covenant" with him. Neither should Job, the man of God, and Job's companions make a banquet with him or part with him among the merchants (vs. 6). In other words, do not partake of all the goods (the best foods, etc.) Leviathan offers you, and do not traffic these luxurious and desirable things among the merchants. That is, don't become rich by commercialism, which is the Devil's doing.

Compare this with the words of Rabbi Higger who, in *The Jewish Utopia*, waxes eloquently about how the Jews partake of the best foods etc., and will enjoy the feast made possible by Leviathan. God also tells Job that the "hope" of Leviathan is in vain (vs. 9). Though he is strong and fierce, his heart is firm as a stone, and all who see him are struck with fear; yet God will eventually destroy Leviathan (vs. 11). No one but God can do so.

Moreover, the key to understanding how diabolical and evil is this beast, Leviathan, is found in *Job, Chapter 41*, where we are told that from the sea beast or serpent, Leviathan, a "light" emanates (vs. 10). Lucifer, in *Isaiah 14*, presents himself as the "bright and the morning Star," or light, i.e. the sun of the morning, the sun being worshipped in all the ancient Mystery Religions. In *Job* we are further told that "His eyelids are like the eyelids of the morning" (vs. 18), and that, "He maketh a path to shine after him" (vs. 32).

The Jewish people, according to Rabbi Higger, follow this path given to them by their "god of light," Lucifer, or Leviathan, the "bright and the morning star." Indeed, his eyes behold their efforts and are upon them as they accomplish their great work, setting up their coming, sinister gulag world of suffering and deceit.

The Oroboros: King Over the Children of Pride

We find that God's Word totally contradicts the Rabbis' joyous account of what wonderful glories await the righteous (the Jews) when the Jewish Utopia is realized. Higger describes the Jews' Holy City, Jerusalem, as having outer walls covered by the skin of the Serpent, which shines a light and beckons to the whole world. Imagine a circular wall compassing a city made up or covered by serpent skin emitting serpentine rays beaming outward. Is this not a vision of the Oroboros serpent encircling and biting its own tail? Inside its circle is the Great City, Jerusalem, city of the Jewish People, its Chosen, whose devilish religion comes to us disguised as a philosophy of wisdom and enlightenment (light). However, this illumination clearly is designed to deceive the people of planet earth.

How utterly prideful are these would-be kings, the Jews. Their King, the crowned Serpent, their god of light and illumination, is in fact king over all the children of pride. God says so, for we read of Leviathan in *Job 41:34:*

> *"He (Leviathan) beholdeth all high things: he is a king over all the children of pride."*

This gigantic serpent of Judaic enlightenment also exercises police state and martial power in order to subdue his victims. "Charmed" by the magic of Judaism, America and the other western nations use their military prowess to advance the cause of Zionism. Their armed forces invade and occupy one nation after another on behalf of the Serpent People. *Job (Chapter 41)* describes this as dragon power—symbolically, burning lamps and sparks of fire go out of

An old Jewish tombstone in a cemetery showing Leviathan crowned as King and Messiah of the Jews.

Leviathan's mouth. Out of his nostrils go smoke and a flame. Indeed this beast is both a dragon and a serpent. And we are reminded again of that passage in the book of *Revelation* which describes the fall of Satan from Heaven:

> *"And the great dragon was cast out, that old serpent, called the Devil, and Satan, which deceiveth the whole world: he was cast out into the earth, and his angels were cast out with him."*
>
> *—Revelation 12:9*

Their Plan—To Rule the Earth

It is that same repulsive being, Satan, the Devil, also known as the Serpent, Leviathan, and the Dragon, which Israel's power-mad rabbis and political leaders are depending on to destroy their enemies, vanquish the nations and install their *"Sovereign Lord of All the World"* (see *The Protocols of the Learned Elders of Zion*) on the throne of world power. He is their would-be redeemer. But what does God say about their foul plan? What of this Leviathan with whose light the Jews boast they shall someday enlighten the world?

I'm afraid the rabbis have a big surprise in store. They would have been much better off to have studied the books of the Old Testament and the prophecies of the New Testament all these centuries than the hoary, stale books of the Talmud and Kabbalah. And they should have listened to their Prophets rather than the ignorant, lustful rabbinical sages of Talmudic tradition. Isaiah, for example, had the answer to Israel's future and the destiny of the Jewish People who bow down to Leviathan expecting favor from the Serpent God. *Isaiah (Chapter 26:21; 27:1)* prophesied the end of the matter, declaring:

> *"For, behold, the Lord cometh out of his place to punish the inhabitants of the earth for their iniquity...*
>
> *"In that day the Lord with his sore and great and strong sword shall punish Leviathan the piercing serpent, even Leviathan that crooked serpent; and he shall slay the dragon that is in the sea."*

And what of Jerusalem, the great city which Higger and the other Zionist rabbis claim shall become the capital and world headquarters of their serpent-inspired Jewish Utopia? In John's vision given him by God while the Apostle was on the isolated and lonely island of Patmos where he had been banished, we find that the Lord in no way considers this place a holy or sacred city. The Jews virtually make of Jerusalem a talisman or idol, but in the book of *Revelation*, the Lord flatly says that this city and its people, to him, are so wicked and vile that He gives the last days city of Jerusalem the sordid spiritual name, *"Sodom and Egypt" (Revelation 11:8).*

Abbadon Comes Up Out of the Pit

In doing so, God reminds us that this is the ungodly city "where also our Lord was crucified" (*Revelation 11:8*) and, moreover, is the wicked city from which "the beast that ascendeth out of the bottomless pit" comes up on the face of the earth to make war with the witnesses of God (*Revelation 11:7*). That, as we have seen, would be Leviathan, though the book of *Revelation* says that he also has other names—he is the king of the bottomless pit and in the Greek language is named *Apollyon* and in the Hebrew, *Abbadon.*

Now Abaddon in Hebrew means "Destroyer." It also

means "Father of Dan." Dan was one of the 12 sons of Jacob and leader of the Tribe of Dan, one of the 12 tribes of ancient Israel. On his deathbed, Jacob gave a prophecy to each of the 12 sons.

The prophecy for Dan was grim: "Dan shall judge his people, as one of the tribes of Israel. Dan shall be a serpent by the way, an adder in the path, that biteth the horse heels, so that his rider shall fall backward."

In fact, the Scriptures show that Dan was greedy and warlike. He lusted for additional territory and took it by force. Each of the twelve tribes was assigned an ensign, or symbol, for its flag. Knowing Dan's wicked nature, Dan was assigned the *serpent* as his tribe's ensign. Angered, Dan refused to accept this and instead chose for himself and his tribe the *eagle*, symbol of divine power and of God's majesty. Dan was blasphemously claiming for himself the right to be honored as God on earth.

Not surprisingly, considering this unbecoming history, in the book of *Revelation*, in *Chapter 7*, we find 12,000 out of each of the 12 tribes of Israel that are sealed as servants of God. But Dan's tribe is not among them, the 12 that are sealed. So we see that Dan's "father" is Satan, the serpent, the king of the bottomless pit whose name in the Hebrew tongue is Abaddon.

We discover that in the deeper teachings of the Kabbalah, the rabbis confide that the king who shall arise in the days to come to reign and rule over the earth as the "Sovereign Lord of All the World" shall come from the tribe of Dan. Dan the serpent—from his bloodline will arise the king of Earth. He will oversee the Jewish Utopia. He it is who shall sit in place of Leviathan in the throne at Jerusalem. Thus, prophecy shall be fulfilled.

The beast nation that crucified Jesus, Israel, was destroyed by Titus in 70 AD and its people dispersed throughout the civilized world, was surely wounded, but its wound was healed. Israel again became a nation in 1948, in disobedience to God which had declared it should be left desolate.

It is, in fact, left *spiritually desolate* and destitute of morals and standards.

Nevertheless, though spiritually bankrupt, Israel has again become a nation. And so astonished is the whole world at this marvelous recovery of the beast's wound that the nations now, universally, pay homage to it and to its inhabitants who spiritually are the Synagogue of Satan. As we read in the prophecy of *Revelation 13*:

> *"And I stood upon the sand of the sea, and saw a beast rise up out of the sea...*
>
> *"and the dragon gave him his power, and his seat, and great authority.*
>
> *"And I saw one of his heads as it were wounded to death; and his deadly wound was healed: and all the world wondered after the beast.*
>
> *"And they worshipped the dragon which gave power unto the beast: and they worshipped the beast, saying, Who is like unto the beast? who is able to make war with him?*
>
> *"...and power was given him over all kindreds, and tongues, and nations."*

The Evil of the Jews

The Leviathan brings to the Jews a radically different

understanding of how they should conduct their lives. The Jew is encouraged to do good works but also to do evil works. Both good and evil are part of Judaism. God is two-faced, Janus-like, and so must be the Jew who venerates the Serpent. Evil is the flip side of God. God is both evil and good, and Jews emulate Him. Redemption may be achieved either through sin or by doing good. Since evil is more pleasurable and more enjoyable, why not do evil?

The Kabbalah teaches that the Messiah can be induced to come by one of two ways. The first way is for the Jews to be very evil and make the earth evil. The second way is for the Jews to be totally good. The first way is the easiest and is thus preferred. Thus, the wise Jew strives to do evil.

Jewish rabbi David Cooper states that even Satan has a divine spark. He is eligible for redemption. The Jew's job is not to eradicate evil or Satan, but to build him up, to help in Satan's redemption. (David Cooper, *God is a Verb: Kabbalah and the Practice of Mystical Judaism*, 1997) The *Zohar* says that, "evil has a divine nature."

Jews are inspired to sin so that evil will be redeemed and *Tikkun Olam* (the mending or restriction of earth) may be accomplished faster. Holiness is attained by sin. Satanic practices such as sexual perversions, theft, robbery, etc. are "bad" but will produce good. Obviously this is a doubleminded religion designed by satanic pyschopaths.

The End to Come in One Hour

And yet, the recovery of Israel as a modern-day rogue nation is not the end of things, but is only a remarkable marker in the history of evil's progress.

Having achieved what they so long schemed and plotted, the satanic Jews shall suffer a staggering truth—that their Jewish Utopia and rule over "all kindreds, and tongues, and nations," is but a fleeting and transient event. Finally, in one hour the Jews' Zionist Kingdom shall come to an ignominious and catastrophic end. And God shall send an angel down from heaven to announce her (the beast city and world empire of the Jews, code-named "Mystery Babylon the Great") great fall *(Revelation 18:1,2,8-10)*:

> *"And after these things I saw another angel come down from heaven, having great power; and the earth was lightened with his glory.*
>
> *"And he cried mightily with a strong voice, saying, Babylon the great is fallen, is fallen, and is become the habitation of devils, and the hold of every foul spirit, and a cage of every unclean and hateful bird....*
>
> *"Therefore shall her plagues come in one day, death, and mourning, and famine; and she shall be utterly burned with fire: for strong is the Lord God who judgeth her.*
>
> *"And the kings of the earth, who have committed fornication and lived deliciously with her, shall bewail her, and lament for her, when they shall see the smoke of her burning,*
>
> *"Standing afar off for the fear of her torment, saying, Alas, alas, that great city Babylon, that mighty city! for in one hour is thy judgment come."*

Judgement will have come. The eyes of Leviathan the piercing serpent will close and open no more. And the anguishing cries of those who once tormented the inhabitants of earth and caused so much trouble and bloodshed will be overwhelmingly loud as they wail and lament their fate in hell. And the dead in Christ shall rise and weep no more. And the whole world shall smile as the Light of Heaven envelops and surrounds them. And the world will be as one.

THREE

The Serpent: Messiah and Redeemer of the Jews

What is the name of the "God" of Judaism? Most Christians believe it to be simply "God," the "Lord," or as given to Moses in *Deuteronomy*, the Great "I Am." Others may suggest Jehovah, Adonai, or perhaps the Tetragrammaton "YHWH." In fact, all these names are intermittently used by people to refer to the Jewish Deity, but none are fully acceptable in Judaism.

Strangely, Jews use a "negative theology" in referring to Deity. A Jew does not use a *revealed* name, but rather a *concealed* name. In Judaism, one does not say what God is, but what he is not. To the Jew, as explained in the Kabbalah, God is therefore generally called *Ein Sof*, which means *"nothingness," "boundless,"* or the *"infinite."*

In effect, God's essence is impenetrable. He cannot be named. He is unknowable, unexplained, a mystery. God has no composition, no attribute; he is ineffable.

This idea of God as being unknowable and unreachable was articulated by the famous Jewish rabbinical sage

Maimonides (1135-1204), who, in his work, *Guide for the Perplexed*, wrote:

> "God's existence includes no composition, and we do not comprehend his essence. Consequently, it is a fake assumption to hold that he has any positive attribute."

God's Name Forbidden

The Social Culture Jewish Newsgroup (online URL: www.scjfag.org) explains that Jews are forbidden to say aloud the name of their God. "Jews consider it sinful to pronounce the name of God." All denominations of Judaism teach that the name of God is forbidden to be uttered except by the High Priest, in the Temple. Since the Temple is no longer existent, the name is never pronounced in religious rituals by Jews. Orthodox Jews never pronounce it for any reason.

In fact, when referring to God, observant Jews use only the word "shmo," which means "His name," or literally, "the name of Him."

"Many Jews conversationally call God by the title, 'Ha Shem,' which is Hebrew for name. Many Jews also write 'G-d' instead of God."

The Kabbalah teaches that *Ein Sof*, whom no one can know, talk to or communicate with, and who has no emotions, has withdrawn from our world. This makes him a *concealed deity*. But Ein Sof does emit, or emanate, rays of light. These *"sparks,"* or bits of light, are assigned various tasks, some of which are sacred or holy. These sparks themselves function as male and female deities, or gods.

According to the Kabbalah, in the Tree of Life there are many such sparks of light functioning as gods and goddesses. Jews can and do often communicate with these deities, being unable to directly reach "God," or "Ein Sof."

Therefore, unlike Christians, who view themselves as priests in direct and full communication with God Almighty, Jews do not talk with God. They do not intercede for others. That is impossible. The Jew believes his life, his works, however, *reflect* Ein Sof, that is, God, here on earth. "God," then, is an *egregore*, a concept, but is not personal. He cannot be loved. He loves not. He has no feelings.

Wikipedia quotes the *Zohar*, the main book of the Kabbalah, as follows:

> "Before He gave any shape to the world, before he produced any form, He was alone, without form and without resemblance to anything else. Who then can comprehend how he was before the creation? Hence it is forbidden to lend him any form or similitude, or even to call Him by His sacred name... God so transcends human understanding as to be practically nonexistent."

Indeed, the Hasidic sect of Judaism believes there is yet another formless mass *beyond Ein Sof*, called *Atzmus*, that is beyond finite/infinite duality. A famous rabbi, the Baal Shem Tov, taught that the *reflection* of Atzmus is found only in Jewish observances and prayer. Judaism is not, therefore, a religion of faith, but of works. Moreover, it is a religion only of, by, and for Jews. Jews are in a distinct and superior class.

Freemasonry's Lost Word

The Masonic Lodge, a Judaic sect, also incorporates this same Deity in its religious doctrine. The new Mason is told only that the "God" of the Lodge is called the *"Great Architect of the Universe."* However, the Word that is God's true name is said to be *"Lost."*

In the third degree the Mason is given a substitute name for the *Lost Word*. That name is "Mahabone." Still later, in the Royal Arch degree, the Mason is told the name of God should never be pronounced by an individual, but is *Jahbulon* (Jah-bul-on). Jahbulon is claimed to be a composite of three deities: Jehovah, Baal, and On, the Egyptian God.

Then, in the 17th degree, the Mason is told that the *Sacred Word* is *Abaddon.* Abaddon happens to be the beast, or dark angel, who leads the demons up out of the bottomless pit in the last days *(Revelation 9 and 11)*. He is the "Sacred Word," holy to the Masons.

Finally, in the higher, 32nd degree, it is revealed to the hapless Masonic initiate that the Lost Word is *Equilibrium*, or *Harmony*, which results when Order is established out of Chaos *(Ordo Ab Chao)*. He is also told that Lucifer is the God to be worshipped and that the "holy trinity" of the ancients represents Lucifer, who is the inverse, good God as compared to the cruel and angry God, Jehovah.

The Holy Serpent: Leviathan Rising

The Kabbalah speaks of two spheres, or regions in which these holy sparks of light—called gods and goddesses and by other names—operate. One is higher, the other lower. The lower region is inhabited by unredeemed man. This is the bottomless pit, a watery abyss or churning sea. Also inhabiting this watery abyss is the *Holy Serpent*, another spark sent by and representing *Ein Sof.*

The Holy Serpent, named *Leviathan*, is Ein Sof's agent, his Angel of help for man. He is placed in the bottomless pit with the ultimate goal of protecting the Jew, advancing him in supernal consciousness, and helping him to rise up out of the bottomless pit.

Whereas, in the Christian faith, the Serpent is called the Dragon and the Devil, he is a negative being, evil and totally separate and apart from God. In Judaism, the unisexual (both male *and* female) Serpent is a Positive Agent, a tool and facilitator for God and a medicine of sorts for man.

As Professor Israel Shahak notes in his classic Jewish textbook, *Jewish History, Jewish Religion*, Jews favorably look upon the Serpent as a companion, friend and guide. They even pray to him. In some cases Jews call on the Serpent to do certain tasks for them, such as the binding, or even death, of an enemy. This is sanctioned in the Talmud.

Is Leviathan, The Holy Serpent, the "Jewish Messiah?"

Edward Hendrie, in his excellent volume, *Bloody Zion: Refuting the Jewish Fables That Sustain Israel's War Against God and Man*, reveals this teaching of the Kabbalah regarding the Serpent:

> "The Cabala (or, Kabbalah) further teaches that the 'holy serpent' is surrounded by evil spirits and she is tempted at all times. The 'holy serpent' is trying to set herself free from the bottomless pit. Once she does this, she can enter the earth as 'the Messiah.'"

In other words, the Holy Serpent is the Jewish Messiah, their Redeemer. He will uplift the Jewish people (the nation known as the "People of the Serpent") to godhood. The Holy Serpent thus represents the Ein Sof and is the Positive Agent who uses "creative destruction" to destroy and rebuild the earth, elevating Jews as the rulers of the planet. This process is known as *Tikkun Olam*, the mending or repair of earth.

The Gentiles, meanwhile, will transfer all their wealth to the Jews and become slaves to Jewish masters. That is their pitiful destiny and the Holy Serpent will see to it that this destiny is achieved. This will occur on what is termed the *Day of Purification*.

The Feast of Leviathan

The Jews, blessed by their Holy Serpent, will live prosperously and in health forever as gods of earth, the Holy Serpent being their guarantor and protector. On the Day of Purification, the Jews will all celebrate their ascension as kings on earth by conducting a gigantic "Feast of the Beast," the Beast, of course, being Leviathan.

On this happy occasion, the assembled Jews will actually serve the Leviathan Beast himself on the menu. He will be cut into pieces and his meat will serve as primary food for the Jews. Bread also shall be served *(Mammon shabbat Leshem, Bereishit 1:21)*.

This is a monstrous mocking of the Christian's Marriage Supper of the Lamb and of the Lord's last meal during Passover. Jesus, we read in *Luke 22:19-20*, "…took bread, and gave thanks, and brake it, and gave unto them, saying, This is my body which is given for you: this do in remembrance of me. Likewise also the cup after supper, saying, This cup is the new testament in my blood, which is shed for you."

The Jews, mocking Christ and his last Eucharist, or communion, consume not the body and blood of Christ, but the meat of Leviathan, the Serpent. The Serpent is to the Jews what Christ Jesus is to Christians. Could a religion be more depraved and more destitute of holiness than is

Judaism?

In consuming the Beast, known to them as their friend, helpmate, and benefactor—their very *Messiah*—the Jews in turn *become* the Beast. The Jews collectively are the Holy Serpent, the most wicked People and entity on earth. Their Kabbalah, the sacred words of their rabbinical sages, says they are *Chosen* for this destiny and fate. Thus, we find that their "man-made traditions," as Jesus termed them, are given ultimate aim. The Jews are, indeed, collectively the Holy Serpent. They are Lucifer incarnate, the occult god of promised freedom and liberty. Unshackled, their motto is: *"Do as thou wilt."*

Worshipping the Serpentine Deity

Dr. Chika Flint, pastor and teacher from Massachusetts and a Christian student of the Kabbalah, speaks of the role of Leviathan in the coming world, or Utopia, of the Jews:

> "God gives the Righteous (Jews) serpentine protection through the magical ability to summon serpents from the lower regions to come and do their bidding. Ultimately, say the rabbis, through supernatural magic, Leviathan himself will take up their cause, encircle the earth, destroy their enemies, and finally serve both as Light of the World and as covering (defender) for the Holy city of Jerusalem." *(Chika Flint, online sermon and paper, "Examining Judaism and the Origin of the Six-Pointed Star," December 18, 2011).*

Dr. Flint warns that the Jews, in fact, literally are worshipping the Serpent, viewing him as holy and as their god:

> "The Judaic religion, in its kabbalistic aspects, literally advocates and practices veneration, admiration, and worship of the Serpentine Deity."

This, reminds Dr. Flint, is exactly what Jesus had declared to the Jews was the case, based on their religion which, said Christ, was not of God but was based on the "traditions of the elders."

Jesus, did in, fact define the Jews. He told us of their destiny and fate. He even told the Pharisees direct to their face what they were—and as we have seen in their kabbalistic objective—what they are to become. He flatly stated:

> *"Ye serpents, ye generation of vipers, how can ye escape the damnation of hell?" (Matthew 23:33)*

Pure Mystery Babylon

The Kabbalah is pure Mystery Babylon religion. It is the religion adopted by the Jews as captives in Babylon during the times of Daniel, combined with their mystical interpretation of the Torah. Rabbi Gershom Solomon (1897-1982), noted Professor of Kabbalah at Hebrew University in Jerusalem, says that the Kabbalah explains the art of devil invocation and explores black magic rituals. Devils, he says, are in submission to the Kabbalah.

The ultimate secret of Kabbalah, its great power, is its revelation that the Holy Serpent is the God to be worshipped and venerated. He will install a Messiah possessed by his spirit, a New King David, on the throne of a renewed Israel. This new potentate will be King of Zion, while the Jews collectively will be gods on earth.

The new King David will not, however, be Christ or God. The Jews are under the impression that *they* will collectively become their own Messiah. Their chief rabbis, forming the Sanhedrin and under the reign of Messiah, will make binding legal and religious decisions. As Jesus told the Jews, "Full well ye reject the commandment of God, that ye may keep your own tradition" *(Mark 7:9)*.

The Jews will soon discover just what a tragic mistake their acts of self-government are, when the Beast of prophecy, the Holy Serpent, one day tires of his subterfuge and declares himself, "God and above all gods" *(II Thessalonians 2)*.

The Jews today respond to Jesus' accusation in arrogant language, flouting their supposed chosen status, and embracing the Holy Serpent, openly declaring:

> "The Holy Serpent is the fountainhead, root and essence for all God's sacred, revelatory Light from which emanates all dimensions of reality...This ray of Light becomes the supernatural pathways of the image of the elongating Serpent who stretches out on both sides with its tail in its head, returning upon its shoulders." (Rabbi Schlomo Eliyashov, *Sifra Di Ztenuta*, Chapter 1 and *Leshem Shevo VeAchlama*)

The Jews rejoice that, in the Kabbalah, they are told that the Ein Sof, their unknowable and ineffable "God," has placed them in the very belly of the Serpent (Rabbi David Bakst, *Journey to the Center of the Torah: The Secret in the Serpent's Belly*, www.chazonhatorah.org). *The Zohar's Book of Concealment* says that there, in the belly of the Holy

Serpent, the Jews are protected from the evil "God" of the Christians and from the tempting demon spirits that are said to constantly assail them. Eventually, the Holy Serpent will rise up, emerging from out of the bottomless pit, and redeem the Jews. Then shall come the wondrous and celebratory *Feast of the Beast*.

FOUR

The Feast of Leviathan: When the Mother of Israel is Ritually Sacrificed and the People of the Serpent Become as Gods

The Feast of the Beast

"The Lord, finally, will prepare a feast for the upright (the Jews). He has salted the huge Leviathan and has prepared the best food, fruit, fish, and meat. The feast will be limitless."

—Leo Schaya
The Universal Meaning of the Kabbalah (1971 ed.)

"And Jesus said unto them, I am the bread of life: he that cometh to me shall never hunger; and he that believeth on me shall never thirst... and the bread that I will give is my flesh, which I will give for the life of the world."

—Jesus Christ
John 6:35-51

The *Protocols of the Learned Elders of Zion* speaks of a Symbolical Snake, or Zionist Serpent (Oroboros) that will conquer every nation on earth and make possible a New World Order, or Jewish Utopia, ruled by the Jews, collectively the world's Messiah and King-Despot. The fact that this same Snake/ Serpent, also called the Dragon, is a central focus of the *Zohar*, the principal book of the Jews' Kaballah, is significant. If the Protocols are a hoax or forgery, how did its authors know of this hidden doctrine of the Kabbalah, which, until recently, was guarded and concealed both from Gentiles and from Jews at large. The Kabbalah's Divine Serpent, the Leviathan, matches up in every way with the *Protocols of Zion's* Symbolical Snake.

The Jews' symbolical Dragon and Serpent of Wisdom, having traversed and conquered the nations of earth, will have made Israel the sole possessor of the Kingdom. All its material wealth shall be theirs. Its treasures of precious metals and gems will have been heaped together in Jerusalem, their capital and world headquarters. Their Holy One, the new King David, the incarnation of the serpent Leviathan, will sit on the throne. He will go into the rebuilt Temple and declare that he is "God" and above all gods (see *II Thessalonians 2*).

The Kabbalah records this jubilant event when the redemption of the Jews, the Righteous, has come. On that day, writes Rabbi Michael Higger in his classic book on Jewish prophecy, *The Jewish Utopia*, the Holy Serpent, Leviathan, will be slain and will be meat at a feast table in Jerusalem. This great feast will be the counterfeit of the wedding and banquet of the Bride of Christ, mentioned by Jesus in the New Testament. In earthly Jerusalem, say the rabbis, there will be the Feast of Leviathan.

The Two Beasts

As in all occult philosophies, the Kabbalah teaches that there are *two* Leviathans, a male and a female. The female, symbolically the Virgin, is the one to be slain, while the masculine Leviathan beast, the survivor of the conflict of opposites, will live and so be honored as Deity. His spirit will possess and energize the King-Despot of the Jews.

The concept of two Leviathans, a masculine and a feminine, is confusing, but then, the Kabbalah's books are purposely intended to be confusing. Their author is Satan, and he is called the "Author of Confusion." It is humorous perhaps, though maybe not surprising, that in the Greek isles in the ancient era, the peoples worshipped a god they called *Typhon*; he was known as the god of confusion!

In Egypt he was called *Seth*, and was one of the gods the children of Israel worshipped in the desert after leaving Egypt. This worship greatly angered the true God in Heaven.

That the Jews honor a feminine as well as a masculine Serpent deity is a fact, though I have never met a single Christian theologian or minister who has one iota of knowledge about this strange and curious doctrine. In Leo Schaya's *The Universal Meaning of Kabbalah*, it is explained that the secret doctrine of Kabbalah and the Jews posits a *trinity* of "Father, Mother, and Son" (Schaya calls it "the supreme and mysterious tri-unity"). This is the same as in all the ancient Mystery Religions, as well as in Hinduism and other occult sects and religions today.

The Mother, moreover, has *two* aspects. According to Schaya, in the Kabbalah we discover that she is called *Malkuth*.

"As passive and receptive principle she is called

The Kaballah teaches that Leviathan has two forms, male and female, one often called Behemoth. Here we find Leviathan as Oroboros, the encircling serpent.

> the 'woman' or the 'wife,' the 'queen' of the divine king...She is called the Power Mother... and the 'daughter,' and *'virgin'* of Israel. She represents the...divine revelation. She is called Shekhinah, the immanence or real presence of God."

The Sacrificed Leviathan Will be Eaten by the Jews

The slain Virgin is the *sacrifice* to be consumed by the high priests and initiates—the man-gods of Zion. Parts of the slain Leviathan will be distributed to the merchants to be sold to the devotees' of the beast. The choicest meats will be reserved for the high priests and consumed at the feast. By eating a "god," they themselves become god. This is a longstanding occult principle.

The skin of the gigantic, slain Leviathan is perceived by the Kabbalists to provide covering and protection for the Jewish people. It shall be placed inside, on the walls of their homes. The Kabbalah says that the skin of the Leviathan will also go on the outer walls of the Great City, Jerusalem. Emitting a supernatural light, the skin (or covering), will beckon and draw all men to Jerusalem, the Holy City of Leviathan and the divine Jews. They are to be seen and honored as the Light of the World, the spiritual role models for all of humanity.

The Regeneration of the Beast

In the ancient Mystery Religions, the serpent was thought to be a divine creature able to regenerate, or renew himself by the shedding of his skin. Likewise, the Jewish Kingdom that is said to once have thrived and prospered under the wise leadership of Kings Solomon and David will have been renewed, regenerated. To the surprise and shock of the Gentiles, Israel shall rise like the Phoenix to become again the premier nation among the lesser heathen. The Nation that put Jesus Christ to death on the cross will be revived, blasphemously promoting Satan's Kingdom across the globe.

Once again, this is pictured in the amazing prophetic book of *Revelation (Chapter 13)* in the New Testament.

> *"And I saw a beast rise up out of the sea...and upon his heads the name of blasphemy...and the dragon*

> *gave him his power, and his seat, and great authority.*
>
> *"And I saw one of his heads as it were wounded to death; and his deadly wound was healed: and all the world wondered after the beast.*
>
> *"And they worshipped the dragon, which gave power unto the beast, saying, Who is like unto the beast? Who is able to make war with him?"*

"The beast rises up out of the sea," says John the Apostle. Is this earthly Israel, the nation that the rabbis say shall rule over humanity in the world to come, a Golden Age in which the Jewish Utopia will rise and be exalted, as taught in the Talmud and Kabbalah?

The Beast is given his power, his seat, and great authority by the dragon, Satan. Indeed, in the Kabbalah, it is Leviathan who conquers the whole world on behalf of his Chosen People, after which they rule and reign by dint of his power, having "great authority" over the Gentiles, who, in the future world, are to be servants of the Jews.

"And I saw one of his heads as it were wounded to death; and his deadly wound was healed: and all the world wondered after the beast." In 70 AD, as prophesied by Jesus, Jerusalem and Israel were invaded and destroyed by Roman General Titus. The survivors fled or were taken captive and dispersed throughout the world. This was the Diaspora, and, astonishingly, their dispersion and resettlement among other peoples and inside other nations actually strengthened the Jews and made of them a great nation—a unified nation within the nations!

The Spirit of Mammon

Blessed by their secret god, Leviathan, and consumed by the spirit of mammon—an inordinate lust for money—the Jews have over the centuries conspired together to defraud the Gentiles and financially advance their own kind. By stealth and deceit they have taken over the nations one-by-one, including the great empires of Europe and Germany, of the U.S.S.R., the British Commonwealth, and the United States and the Americas. Through banking and fiat money systems, their money barons and lords, the Rothschilds, now rule over many.

Having heaped up treasure for Leviathan, the "God of Forces," the Zionist Jews now covertly rule over the largest domain ever assembled and are dominant over most of the world's peoples. Surely, they are blessed by Leviathan. *The wound inflicted by the Romans in 70 AD is healed, and all the eyes of the world are focused on the tiny nation of Israel in the Middle East.* It is, perhaps the head of the beast, but its serpentine body now encircles the whole globe.

Oroboros lives. The beast's wound, once believed to be deadly, is healed. His power over the nations, thanks to his proxies, is mighty, and everywhere there exists a pallid "fear of the Jews" and what they might do to you if they perceive you as their enemy. As the scriptures say, all the people of earth in unison, now ask, *"Who is like unto the beast? Who is able to make war against him?"* Does not all the world look in awe and wonder at his military and intelligence prowess?

Can Egypt, can Iraq, Lebanon, Syria, and Afghanistan successfully make war against Israel and its western allies? In 1917, even the mighty Czar of Russia was overcome by the Jews who masqueraded as Bolsheviks and Communists.

In 1945, Hitler and Germany succumbed. “Who is able to make war with the beast?”

“And They Worshipped the Beast”

Yet, the beast, Israel, wants more than mere acquiescence by conquest. It wants worship. For we read: *“And they worshipped the beast.”* The *Feast of the Beast* is the symbolic event that will someday very soon celebrate the coming of Leviathan and the ascension to divinity of the Jewish people who, collectively, shall be their own Messiah and Lords over a global kingdom: The “*Jewish Utopia*.” Such an event the world will never before have witnessed and it is at that moment that the Leviathan, the piercing serpent of *Job 41*, will take the throne of King David and demand worship of every inhabitant on the planet.

It was Thomas Hobbes’ famous novel, *Leviathan*, that encapsulates and epitomizes in prosaic language the spirit of the beast as pictured in the Kabbalah. Now Hobbes was a Christian and quite possibly he did not and could not envision the Jewish idea of the perfect, mended world to come, when the Jews would lord it over all mankind, reigning with their god, the serpent and dragon, with a rod of iron. Yet strangely, it was Thomas Hobbes who set forth the idea and concept that people, left to their own devices, their lives being short in span and brutish, and being in a constant, perpetual state of fear, violence, and war and being desperate for resolution, should vastly improve their lot by joint contract, or *covenant*.

This would be the solution to their horrid problems—for each to voluntarily surrender their freedom to other men through a pact or covenant. And once their freedoms have been voluntarily circumscribed, once they have been transferred to the politics or people at large, their covenant cannot be revoked.

Leviathan, the beast rising up out of the sea (*Job 41* and *Revelation 9*). Frontis piece for Hobbes' classic book.

Thus, by *covenant*, Hobbes surmises, is created Leviathan:

> "...it is a real unit of them all in one and the same person, made by covenant of every man with every man, in such manner as if every man should say to every man: I authorise and give up my right of governing myself to this man, or to this assembly of men, on this condition; that thou give up, thy right to him, and authorise all his actions in like manner. This done, the multitude so united in one person is called a COMMONWEALTH; in Latin, CIVITAS. This is the generation of that great LEVIATHAN, or rather, to speak more reverently, of that mortal god to which we owe, under the immortal God, our peace and defence."

Yes, the Feast of the Beast for the Jews represents the creation on earth of the Commonwealth, or City, of Leviathan. This is a *Great City* that will encompass and govern all the earth. Its circular outer parameters are covered by the male Leviathan beast. Its Capital, Jerusalem, shall have the skin of the Leviathan beast as covering which also shall be for a light unto the world. The meat of Leviathan will be consumed, being derived from the *ritual sacrifice*. The conflict between the unknowable God and the Serpent God shall have been resolved. As the peoples under the dominance of the monarchs once both sorrowfully and joyously cried out upon the death of their king or queen: "The Kind is dead; Long live the King."

In the instance of the redemption of the Jews (their

coronation) the establishment of their throne of the beast, metaphorically the roar of the masses will be heard around the world:

> *"Leviathan is slain. Yet, Leviathan lives!"*

A Ceremonial Ritual Sacrifice

Please note that I described this kabbalistic event prophesied by the Jewish sages to occur in the world to come as the *Feast of the Beast*, which is, in fact, to be a ceremonial *ritual sacrifice*. Though this may seem odd to the uninitiated, I assure you that in the satanic realm, ritual sacrifices are common. In the ancient Mystery Religions, and among the Jews, the worshippers ritually sacrificed animals, humans, or effigies or representatives thereof. Such sacrifices are made today in Santeria and voodoo (even in the U.S.A.) and among India's Hindus, African tribalists, and others. In most cases, the body of the sacrificial victim is consumed by the high priests and the people, the liturgents.

To this day, the Orthodox Jews and their kabbalist cohorts ritually sacrifice chickens, lambs, doves, and other creatures. The rabbis contend that in the world to come, they will once again regularly sacrifice an unblemished heifer cow in their rebuilt Temple in Jerusalem.

Thus, in the Kabbalah, we find the account of the huge beast, Leviathan, being sacrificed and his meat enjoyed by the celebrants. Now as grotesque an image as this may conjure up in our minds, it is perhaps worthy to note that even in traditional Christianity the sacrifice of the body of Jesus Christ our Lord is symbolically offered up. In the Protestant churches, the congregations celebrate *communion*, and the unleavened bread and wine (grape juice in some churches and denominations) represent the flesh and blood

Above: The history of the Jews show many sacrifices made by rabbis and the people. Here we see a modern-day rabbi sacrificing a chicken on Yom Kippur.

Above: In the book of *Amos* we find God angry over the Jews sacrifice of their own children to the demon god, Moloch.

Right: According to a relatively new book by Jewish historian Ariel Toaff, in medieval days the Jews' ritually killed a young Gentile child. They drank the blood.

of Jesus. This is done in remembrance of Him and in honor of His willing sacrifice in our place on the cross of Calvary.

In the Roman Catholic churches, the mass is said to not only commemorate the sacrifice of Jesus on the cross but also is claimed to be the actual flesh and blood of Christ. In consuming these elements, the Catholic faithful believe they are partaking of the *real presence* of his body and blood. Many Protestants, of course, reject this doctrine, maintaining the symbolic memorial to be scripturally correct.

In any event, we can safely assume that at the Feast of the Beast, the image of a ritual of the eating of Leviathan evokes powerful emotions and passions because, in eating the beast (Leviathan the Dragon/Serpent), the Jew adamantly believes himself thereby to be *transformed*. He eats the God. He becomes the God. He, the Jew, is thus himself worthy of worship as God on earth.

Mother of the Community of Israel

Jews worship two mother goddesses. In the Kabbalah, the "lower mother," is the inverse, or mirror image, of the highest mother. The lower mother, *Malkuth*, is found in the darkness—what Christians would call *hell!*—yet the Jewish rabbis who adore their Kabbalah esteem Malkuth as the Supreme Deity. Schaya says she operates from the "luminous" dark side where there is invisible light.

She is "superintelligible" and is the *"Light of the World,"* though she resides *below*, in the "firmament which has no light from itself." She is the very *presence* of God in his feminine reality. She is the "mystical body of Israel," the unity of the Jewish People, the "Bride" of the divine king. She deserves the worship of her supplicants, the Righteous Jews who shall inherit the earth and all matter.

The Kabbalah reveals that the fertile Malkuth receives

the *"divine emanations"* (semen) from this divine king through their holy sex act, and through this influx the cosmos is created. In effect she, Malkuth, is man's creator and is therefore the giver of all good things. Though sexually active in a spiritual sense, she is said to be the *"Virgin daughter of Zion."*

Do the top Jews, the Rothschilds, the Bronfmans, the Reichmanns and all the other billionaire Jewish dynasties really believe these things? *Yes, they do!* Is the Kabbalah and its teachings the province of only a small, fringe group of radical rabbis? *Absolutely not!*

This is the doctrine and spiritual teaching that today governs the conduct and life of Judaism and the religious Jews. Though not every Rabbi accepts and endorses Kabbalism; its theological foundations cannot be separated from the overall body of Talmudic Judaism. In fact, as each day passes, the theology of Kabbalah has a tighter and tighter grip on the minds and souls of both the Jewish elite and the pious.

It is they who manage and superintend world affairs for the Jews. They, the Kabbalists, are the overlords, the master. They give the word, and Israel moves as decreed. Even a cursory examination of Israel's domestic and foreign policies and of the culture and social composition of Jews across the globe provides evidence of this reality. The kabbalists are the captains of Israel's destiny. They hold the keys to the future of Zion.

Rothschild and the Virgin

To emphasize this point, consider the city of Tel Aviv, the financial capital of the state of Israel, the headquarters of its stock market and banks. Founded in 1909 with the money and active support of Baron Edmund Rothschild, this sparkling city on the Mediterranean coast sprang up from the desert sand like a prosperous fruit tree. The very name Tel Aviv means "spring hill."

The city is laid out with streets given names honoring Israel's dignitaries and famous movers and shakers. Theodore Herzl, called the "Father of Zionism," has a street named after him. So does Moses Hess, the Communist pioneer who inspired and was a mentor for Karl Marx. But the most prestigious street, with the most expensive real estate, is *Rothschild Boulevard.*

As you travel down the luxurious, palm-tree laden Rothschild Boulevard, you will come to a plaque over the entrance to Ledenburg House. On that plaque is an inscription which reads in Hebrew:

> "Again I will build you, and you shall be built, virgin daughter of Zion."

This same, telling quote was chosen as a motto for the city crest of Tel Aviv. So here we see in plain view the teachings of the rabbis that guides the Jews adeptly toward their destiny. They are convinced that they are *The Builders* and that they are building a kingdom for the daughter of Zion, the Supreme Mother. This is the superintelligible woman whose holy sexual rite and unity with the divine king endows the Jews with such awesome creative power and is able to first create, then destroy, and then mend, or rebuild, the world (earth) into the mirror image of Heaven. She, Malkuth, the Divine Mother, the Shekhinah, who comes from the darkness but is the light of the world, is the real presence of God and is veritably the "community of Israel." She is further the Bride of Israel, the Holy Virgin, and as co-creators with her, the prideful Jews are building *her*

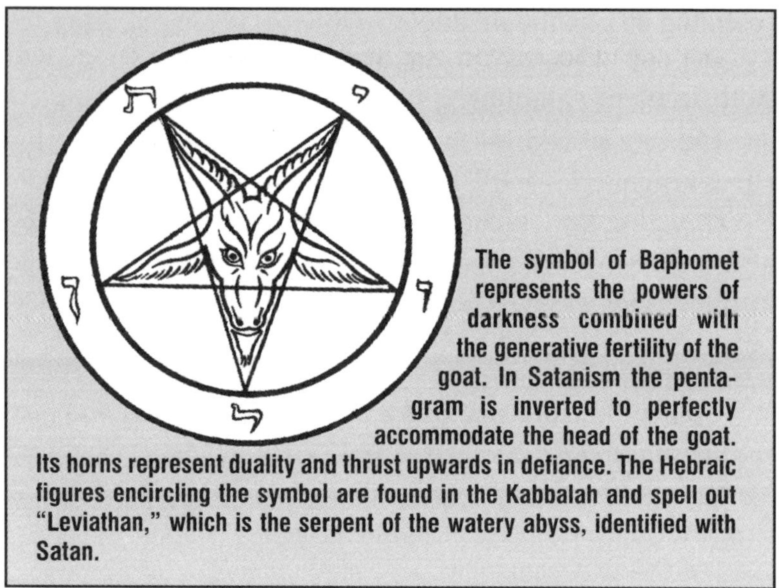

The symbol of Baphomet represents the powers of darkness combined with the generative fertility of the goat. In Satanism the pentagram is inverted to perfectly accommodate the head of the goat. Its horns represent duality and thrust upwards in defiance. The Hebraic figures encircling the symbol are found in the Kabbalah and spell out "Leviathan," which is the serpent of the watery abyss, identified with Satan.

Kingdom.

Leviathan Rising: The Messiah Arrives

The Leviathan that rises out of the sea *(Revelation 13)* is her symbol. Leviathan is the Divine presence, the Serpent/fish that, having risen from the sea, goes on to envelop and conquer the world, in unity with her husband, the Leviathan beast that resides in the wilderness. The banquet, or Feast of the Beast, is dedicated to the feminine Leviathan, and her symbolic body will be consumed at the table. Accompanying this banquet will be the feature attraction—the son of the two Leviathan beasts, the Mother Queen and the Father King. Oh what a miracle-working figure he shall be.

While according to the *Encyclopedia Judaica*, the Jews see themselves allegorically as "Messiah," nevertheless they intend to exalt a living and breathing man-god to reign as the symbolic Serpent/Dragon King of the fulfilled Jewish Utopia. He will be the focal point of their adoration. He shall sit on the throne and judge the nations.

The son who sits on the throne of the new Israel will come from the bloodline of the Tribe of Dan whose ensign is the Serpent. He will bring judgment to his people. And he will give honor to his mother, whom the Jews know as Malkuth. She is the one whom the Prophets of the Old Testament identified as the "Whore of Babylon." The book of *Revelation, Chapter 17*, calls her "Mystery, Babylon the Great, Mother of Harlots and abominations of the earth."

> *"And there came one of the seven angels which had the seven vials, and talked with me, saying unto me, Come hither; I will shew unto thee the judgment of the great whore that sitteth upon many waters:*
>
> *"With whom the kings of the earth have committed fornication, and the inhabitants of the earth have been made drunk with the wine of her fornication.*
>
> *"So he carried me away in the spirit into the wilderness: and I saw a woman sit upon a scarlet coloured beast, full of names of blasphemy, having seven heads and ten horns.*
>
> *"And the woman was arrayed in purple and scarlet colour, and decked with gold and precious stones and pearls, having a golden cup in her hand full of abominations and filthiness of her fornication:*
>
> *"And upon her forehead was a name written, MYSTERY, BABYLON THE GREAT, THE MOTHER OF HARLOTS AND ABOMINATIONS OF THE EARTH.*

"And I saw the woman drunken with the blood of the saints, and with the blood of the martyrs of Jesus: and when I saw her, I wondered with great admiration."

—Revelation 17:1-6

FIVE

The U.S.A. and World Jewry Plunder the World

Leviathan: The Chronicle of the Two Beasts

In the Kabbalah we find the doctrine of an androgynous (combined male and female) "God" consisting of two beasts that work to conquer the whole Gentile world and bring in the Jewish-led kingdom on earth. This is the quest for the *Jewish Utopia*, i.e. the *New World Order*. The two beasts are said to be "Leviathan, the piercing serpent," in both his masculine and feminine forms (or aspects).

The feminine Holy Serpent (Leviathan) rises up out of the churning sea of chaos which is also described as the "hellpot" or bottomless pit. She ascends along with the millions of devils and demonic entities which were with her in the bottomless pit. This feminine Leviathan inexorably makes her way, slithering across and around the planet, conquering all nations and peoples until the circle is complete and the Jews and their Messiah are crowned with glory.

The female Leviathan is honored as the "covering" and glory of Israel. She empowers the people of Israel to become the "Light of the World." She is the very symbol of the "Community of Israel."

The Feast of Leviathan to Inaugurate Golden Age for Jews

Ceremonially, the Kabbalah teaches that the meat of this female Leviathan will be divided and the Jews will eat of it at a great banquet and feast to inaugurate the global Jewish Utopia. This will be a Holy Eucharist ritual at which the "Real Presence" of the Holy Serpent deity is consumed and celebrated.

This painting depicts Satan serving a guest at his decadent feast.

Whereas the book of *Revelation* makes reference to the allegorical "Marriage Supper of the Lamb" in which the saints of God will dine and celebrate victory with their Lord and Saviour, Jesus Christ, this event, at which the Jews as a nation shall be joined to the Holy Serpent and partake of its "flesh and blood," is called in the Kabbalah the *"Feast of Leviathan."* Biblically, we should refer to it as the "Feast of the Beast."

According to the kabbalists, a second divine beast, the masculine aspect of Leviathan, comes up from the earth and resides in the wilderness. This Holy Serpent is protector of Israel and enforcer. His power is great and his size is huge. He mates with the female Leviathan and a Son, a human incarnation of Leviathan, is born. This son is the Messiah of Israel. We note, too, that according to the kabbalist rabbis, the Jewish people collectively are their own Messiah, and yet, they also desire a man to rule over them, to be the new King David (some teach King Solomon). He will be a flesh and blood Messiah, sitting on the throne wearing a symbolic crown. As King of Israel, he will enter the Temple and, the rabbis say, inaugurate the Golden Age of Jewish global sovereignty.

The Two Beasts of Revelation 13

Now the amazing thing about this serpentine doctrine of the Jews and their holy books of Kabbalah is that it exactly parallels the prophecy given to the Apostle John and written in the thirteenth chapter of *Revelation*. There, in *Revelation 13*, we are told of two beasts. The first beast rises up out of the sea. He has seven heads and ten horns, and upon his heads "the name of blasphemy." We are informed by the Scriptures that it is the dragon (Satan) who gives this first beast "his power, his seat, and great authority."

One of the heads of this beast receives a severe injury, “as if wounded to death.” But miraculously, the sea beast does not die, instead, “his deadly wound was healed, and all the world wondered after the beast:”

> *“And they worshipped the dragon which gave power unto the beast: and they worshipped the beast, saying Who is like unto the beast? Who is able to make war with him?”*
>
> *—Revelation 13:4*

The beast that rises up out of the sea is described as having seven heads and ten horns; A “horn” symbolizes power as invested in a nation or as wielded by a leader. We recall that there were initially twelve tribes of Israel, each with a king, prince or ruler. However, because of their wickedness, two of the twelve tribes, those led by Ephraim and Dan, were cast out, leaving ten. Is this the meaning of the “ten horns?”

The Wound is Healed—Israel is Restored in 1948

One of the heads of the first beast of Revelation was grievously wounded. Remarkably, Jerusalem and Israel also suffered a deadly wound in 70 AD when Roman General Titus destroyed the Great City, broke down the Temple, slew hundreds of thousands of its citizens and dispersed the remainder as a troublesome and hateful captive people despised by all the nations.

What’s more, we read in *Revelation 13* that this “deadly wound,” appearing to be so severe an injury that it would be fatal, was nevertheless miraculously healed. The recovery and survival of the wounded beast was so amazing that the world was awestruck, “All the world wondered after (that is, marveled at) the beast." Moreover, they worshipped the dragon (Satan) who had given power unto the beast, and they worshipped the beast, saying, "Who is like unto the beast? Who is able to make war with him?"

Is this not a direct parallel to the history and example of Israel and the Jews? Just as was prophesied by Jesus, the Romans in 70 AD completely destroyed the city of Jerusalem. The Romans' declared purpose was to insure the troublesome, hate-filled Jews would never come back to inhabit the city and rebuild its Temple. But in 1948, after a simmering absence of some 1,870 years, the Jews did return to Palestine. They founded the modern-day nation of Israel that year, and in 1967, less than two decades later, captured Jerusalem and have now made it their ancient and modern capital. As it now stands, the Jews of today have every intent to conspire at every turn to rebuild their blasphemous great Temple. Undoubtedly, we soon shall see that mind-boggling feat take place. The Jews will make it happen.

Was not the wound of the beast (Israel) miraculously healed? Can you name even one other destroyed nation whose people were dispersed across the planet for almost two millennia that refused to assimilate but, rather, increased in worldly (and Satanic) power sufficiently to re-establish itself? True, the modern state of Israel has had a lot of assistance from the U.S., from Britain and France, and from Russia in attaining this objective and in the healing of its "deadly wound." But then again, the Bible prophesied that its power came from Satan, the dragon, and so these other nations are propelled by hellish forces to assist the Jews.

The "Beast" is Worshipped

Today, the Jews and their reborn (healed) nation of Israel are, as prophesied, *"worshipped"* by millions of Christian evangelicals who tremble with emotion as they pay homage to "God's Chosen People." Without regard to the warnings of Jesus and the Apostles found in the New Testament, these "Zionist Christians" glowingly describe the Jews as "the Apple of God's eye." Many send tribute (offerings and donations) to Zionist groups; they support Jewish causes with their time and their money. They demand that their own government—whether it be the United States, Britain, France, Australia, Canada, or New Zealand—provide billions annually in foreign aid assistance to Israel and shower the Israeli defense forces with the latest high tech weapons and military equipment. They jump with joy at the knowledge that Israel has a Goliath-like arsenal of nuclear bombs, missiles, submarines and ships. They celebrate each time Israel attacks and kills its innocent neighbors, the Arabs and Palestinians.

Many evangelical Christians in the U.S. do not hesitate to say that Israel comes first and America second in all things. They see no problem with influential Jews running Washington, D.C. and all other sectors of the economy and culture. They believe it is, in fact, all God's doing. These millions of pseudo-Christians continually express their "love" and admiration for Israel.

Though the Scriptures, in *Revelation 9*, call Israel and Jerusalem in the last days "Sodom and Egypt" and as the "Synagogue of Satan" in *Revelation 2:9* and *3:9*, Christian Judaizers can find no fault at all in Israel's warped, bloody, and prejudiced domestic and foreign policies.

In almost any United States election, whether at the national or local level, candidates of either political party are required by the Judaizer worshippers of Israel to declare that they sincerely "love Israel" and will always put that nation first. At 2008's vice presidential debate, both major party candidates, Senator Joseph Biden and Governor Sarah Palin, made it a point to assure millions of TV viewers they loved and supported Israel and are "Zionists."

It stands to reason that today, after seven decades of receiving untold trillions in military and economic aid from the United States and other Western nations, Israel is superior in might to its potential Middle East foes. Still, each time the well-armed Israelis win a military skirmish or victory in battle against the unarmed Palestinians or the almost defenseless Lebanese, the Christian Judaizers and Israeli admirers swoon in ecstasy and utter those magical words of adoration: "Who is like unto the beast (Zionist Israel)? Who is able to make war with him?"

Blasphemy Against God, War on the Saints

Given such undue respect by many cowardly, ignorant, so-called "Christians" the beast (Israel and World Jewry as led and inspired by Leviathan the Serpent), whose deadly wound is healed, does not hesitate to make maximum use of its filthy and vile mouth to slander, defame, and blaspheme God and His angels in heaven:

> *"And there was given unto him a mouth speaking great things and blasphemies; and power was given unto him...*
>
> *"And he opened his mouth in blasphemy against God, to blaspheme his name, and his tabernacle, and them that dwell in heaven."*
>
> *—Revelation 13: 5-6*

The beast also makes war against Christianity and the people of God:

> *"And it was given to him to make war with the saints, and to overcome them: and power was given him over all kindreds, and tongues, and nations.*
>
> *"And all that dwell upon the earth shall worship him, whose names are not written in the book of life of the Lamb slain from the foundation of the world."*
>
> *—Revelation 13:7-8*

The Judaizer and Zionist Christians have no complaint about the blasphemy of Israel and the Jews. The Jews' most holy book, the Talmud, falsely accuses Jesus of the most heinous of crimes, brands him a fornicator, a magician, a bastard, and worse. Both the Talmud and Kabbalah reek of mind-numbing, utter blasphemy. But the admirers of Israel simply smile and nod approvingly, or else enthusiastically brush aside the whole fabric of Jewish evil. Can these people really be genuine Christians if they are not offended by blasphemy directed against the One whom they claim to worship and adore as "King of Kings and Lord of Lords?"

Guilty of Blasphemy

Emboldened by the fear of those over whom he has hegemony and encouraged by the unlikely worship of so many admirers, especially of those in the Christian world, the kabbalist serpent and beast, the Leviathan that is Israel and the Jews, for almost 2,000 years has never ceased its abominable efforts to blaspheme the name of Christ, to undermine and diminish the authority of the host of heaven, and to make war on true and authentic Christianity. The Talmud and Kabbalah are prime evidence that the Holy Serpent, the beast adored by the Kabbalists as their "god," is the world's chief blasphemer of Jesus Christ.

This definitely fits the prophetic pattern. *Revelation 2* addresses this despicable blasphemy, pointing out that the endtime usurper is known as a blasphemer by God:

> *"I know the blasphemy of them which say they are Jews, and are not, but are the Synagogue of Satan."*

Racial Imposters

Notice that these evildoers "say they are Jews, and are not," indicating very possibly that the Ashkenazi Jews that make up some ninety percent of World Jewry *say* they are "Jews," but in reality, they are racial imposters, having originated not in ancient Israel but in ancient Khazaria and then migrating on into Europe and Russia.

From there, after World War II, funded by the Zionist elite and with the acquiescence of both Moscow and Washington, D.C., they settled in Palestine, bludgeoned and ethnically cleansed that territory, and set up their imposter modern nation of "Israel."

According to the New Testament, even those—a minority—who may come from ancient Israelite DNA are nevertheless not real "Jews." The Apostle Paul taught the truth, that being a Jew and of Israel is not a matter of flesh and blood but of spirit. Thus, not all who claim ("say" they are") Jewish are, in fact, Israel. Only those who believe in Jesus Christ are entitled by spiritual rebirth to citizenry in the "Israel of God" *(Galatians 6)*.

What we discover, then, is that these imposter "Jews" identify themselves as servants of Satan by the very fact that their most holy books, the many volumes of Talmud and Kabbalah, are both sordid, anti-Christian, and filled with blasphemy.

Holy Serpents Male and Female

What we know is that Israel and Jerusalem is unquestionably the first beast of Revelation that rises out of the sea. Judaism and its rabbis teach in their Kabbalah that Leviathan is physical Israel's "symbolic snake," her spiritual covering, her light on her journey toward global domination. But we recall that Judaism and its rabbis also teach that there are two symbolic Leviathan beasts, one rising from the bottomless pit (the sea of chaos), the other residing in the wilderness. So, too, in Christianity's prophetic book of *Revelation*, we are told of this second beast. The first beast, the Scriptures say, rises out of the sea, the second up out of the earth:

> *"And I beheld another beast coming up out of the earth; and he had two horns like a lamb, and he spake as a dragon."*
>
> *—Revelation 13:11*

The Kabbalah teaches that the Jewish deity, the serpent beast Leviathan, resides *"in the wilderness."* In parallel form the book of Revelation speaks of the second beast *"coming up out of the earth."* Thus we have:

- Two beasts described in the Kabbalah, one rising from the sea (the bottomless pit, or abyss), the other dwelling in the wilderness.

- Two beasts described in *Revelation 13*, the first rising up out of the sea, the other up out of the earth.

These parallels are eye-opening. The fact is that again and again we discover that Israel and World Jewry fit the prophetic pattern laid out in the Holy Bible for Satan's endtime system and man of ultimate evil.

America, Britain, and the Two Horns

Revelation tells us that the second beast, rising up out of the earth, "has two horns like a lamb and speaks as a dragon." In biblical symbology a horn is a sign of power. The lamb meanwhile, symbolizes a creature of spiritual purity imbued with love, compassion, meekness, and kindness. Thus, this beast is worldly powerful and also *appears* to be a precious lamb. One wonders if this is not the United States of America, which proceeded out of Great Britain.

The U.S.A. is the world's greatest military superpower and war maker nation, but through propaganda and facile use of the media and diplomacy, it bills itself as a peace-loving nation that desires nothing more than to extend the blessings of Democracy to all the world.

The U.S. kills a lot of people to bring them the "blessings" of Democracy. While portraying itself as a dove, its huge and impressive war machine cuts a huge swath of death and destruction across the Middle East. The United States, with its chief ally, Britain, pretends to be a lamb, but it is not.

What's more, as the history of the U.S.A. gives testimony, this nation does "speak as a dragon." Our diplomats, the Pentagon and our military generals, our intelligence services, and our President and Congress, specialize in dishing out self-serving lies, disinformation and deceptions. Billions of dollars from intelligence "black budgets" are spent annually to "pull the wool" over the planetary masses and that includes a slew of lies and propaganda bellowing out to its own citizens. By now, after decades of lies, the reputation of the U.S government and its many sub-agencies is far beyond redemption. Satan, the Scriptures say, is the "Father of Lies," but surely the United States and Britain, its parent and now co-partner in criminal syndication, can accurately boast that it is at least the "Son of Lies."

The Man With the Number 666

Is the United States, then, the second beast of *Revelation 13*, the one that rises up out of the earth? I am convinced of this fact. The United States is, of course, led by a chief executive, the President, and is the world's greatest superpower nation. As the U.S.A. is the second beast of *Revelation 13*, we find that the man who leads the U.S.A. and is its President will have the number 666:

> *"Here is wisdom. Let him that hath understanding count the number of the beast: for it is the number of a man, and his number is six hundred three score and six (666)."*

The Bible tells us that this second beast is head of resources, so economically and politically powerful that it causes all the world's people to take the mark, or the name, or the number of the beast either in their forehead or in their right hand. The number of the beast is the ominous 666.

Using occult numerology and Gematria we can trace this triple six number all the way back to ancient Babylon, where it represented the Great Goddess. Her worship spread throughout the world, and in the Old Testament, in *Jeremiah*, the prophet revealed that Jewish women would go to the Temple and bake cakes and make sacrifice to the Great Goddess, whom they called the "Queen of Heaven."

In the ancient religions, the Great Goddess had a son, whom the apostate Jews, as well as other nations, worshipped as "Tammuz."

In the Jewish Kabbalah we find that the goddess, *Malkuth*, is Queen and sits on a throne in the bottomless pit. Malkuth is, in fact, Leviathan the Holy Serpent, god and leader of the Jews.

Also, we note that the Star of David, on Israel's flag, is coded 666, having *six* external points, *six* triangles, and containing a *six-sided* hexagram.

Leader of the U.S.A.-Israeli Coalition

So we are told in *Revelation* that the number of the beast, 666, is also the number of a man, whom scholars say will be the antichrist, described as the "Man of Sin" and the "Son of Perdition." As the leader of the U.S.A-Israel coalition, this man will certainly be a Jew, for only a Jew would be permitted to enter a rebuilt Temple of the Jews in Jerusalem (see *II Thessalonians 2*) and declare that he is God and above all other gods. Moreover, the prophet Daniel's vision of this latter day ruler was that of a Jew who would refuse to worship the "God of his fathers" but, instead, would worship a strange god called the "God of Forces."

It stands to reason that the Antichrist, who has the number 666 will be the political leader of the United States, in other words the President. This great nation has long been the sponsor, benefactor, and military proxy for Israel, and today wealthy Jews and Jewish lobby groups are the chief powerbrokers in the aisles of power in America.

As I explained, in regard to the book of *Revelation's* picture of the second beast coming up out of the earth, this would be a striking parallel with the prophecies found in the Kabbalah. In the Kabbalah there are two symbolical snakes or deities: one is female, the other male; the male is of the earth and dwells "in the wilderness."

If we trace the years back to 1492 we find that from the perspective of the civilized world of the Europeans, America was a huge wilderness populated by strange "savages" (native American "Indians"). That is the way Christopher Columbus and his entourage envisioned the lands they discovered. But from this vast New World wilderness, "out of the earth" a powerful nation and empire ascended to the heights of world power. This nation, the United States, has become so powerful that its military might and capability enabled it to lock horns with and militarily defeat the British Commonwealth, Spain, France, Germany, Italy, and many other older advanced nations.

The man who in the last days leads this powerful nation and people dwelling in the New World wilderness will be given great power by Satan, whom the Scriptures call "that old serpent, the Devil and Satan." One of America's earliest and most astonishing symbols was the serpent with its defiant and rebellious message of warning, *"Don't Tread on Me!"*

Star of David Over America's Great Seal

Adopting as its national logo and Great Seal the eagle, a universal symbol of deity and power, the United States, on its currency, over the eagle placed the six-pointed Star of David. The Star sits within a cloud. This indicates the androgenous male/female deity of the Jews—the sexually united Father and Mother Leviathan Serpent. This same God of the Jews is represented by the six-pointed star found on Israel's national flag. This consists of two triangles joined to form the six-pointed star. That is also the star image on America's currency, depicted with a covering of the Shekinah, the divine, feminine cloud of glory.

Thus, the spiritual connection to ancient Israel is made

obvious to those of discernment and with eyes to see. Moreover, this Great Seal of the United States has a reverse side. Why would the Great Seal, or any seal for that matter, *need* a reverse side? Again we see the evidence of the occultic dualism of Judaism and its perverse Mystery religious ideology.

Indeed, the reverse side of the Great Seal of the United States was hidden from the American people until the year 1935, when President Franklin D. Roosevelt, a crypto Jew Zionist and 32nd degree Freemason, ordered the Treasury to redesign the one dollar bill and add this reverse image. In this way, the Zionists and Masons revealed their diabolical plan for a New World Order based on the ancient Luciferian

religion of Egypt. The image is an unfinished pyramid with the eye of the Sun god (Osiris, *aka* Lucifer) hovering in a radiant capstone just above. Underneath is the fascinating Latin inscription, *Novus Ordo Seclorum*, which translated means *New World Order Separate From God*. The Freemasons and other Secret Societies simply refer to the inscription as inferring the "New World Order."

What we have, then, on the most common unit of U.S.

currency, the one dollar bill, is also the Great Seal with an obverse (front) and a reverse (or occult) side. On the dollar bill is the Jews' six-pointed star which came out of Egypt and is unmasked as Satan's mystery symbol by the martyr Stephen in *Acts 7:43*. This star gives honor and glory to the Egyptian and pagan deities. On the left side is displayed yet another Egyptian design, the pyramid, all seeing eye, and a radiant sun capstone, along with the goal of the Satanists, a New World Order, succinctly written in Latin.

How did this Great Seal and its Israel-Egyptian-Luciferian design come to be America's supreme symbol? I explain this and elaborate in some detail in several of my other books, including *Codex Magica—Secret Signs, Mysterious Symbols, and Hidden Codes of the Iluminati*, and therefore will not use this space so as not to be redundant and so that I can include here more pressing information. But I do believe it important to note that in the late 18th century, in the Washington-Franklin-Jefferson era, the ethnic Jewish population in the 13 new states was tiny and insignificant.

The Jews Financed the American Revolution

However, the *moneyed* influence of the Jews was huge, indeed. James Madison and some other founding fathers were showered with "gifts" and "loans" by representatives of European Jewish bankers, Rothschild's agents in America, chief among them. Rothschild's agent, Haym Solomon (or Salomon). Haym Solomon came to the United States colonies in 1774, just two years before the Declaration of Independence and just before hostilities ensued with Britain. Solomon became the *"Financier of the American Revolution,"* and his statue stands today in honor before the entrance to the American Jewish Museum of History, an institution which until recently sat on a valuable and precious piece of land in

Philadelphia directly across the street from the historic, cracked Liberty Bell.

A Common Destiny: U.S.A. and World Jewry Are United

These facts, including the esoteric hidden meaning of the Great Symbol and other images placed on our currency, demonstrate the truism that the United States and World Jewry, to use a cliché, are united at the hip. If the Illuminati succeed in their global quest, the occult destiny of America will be fulfilled simultaneously with the advent of the *Jewish Utopia*. The two beasts of *Revelation* will be as one, and hell on earth will become not a distant and etheric possibility in the minds and lives of men, but a real and present all-encompassing horror.

Now let us see more about this plan of the Jewish-led Illuminati as it relates to the actions of the second beast. The first beast, as we have discovered, is the miraculously healed physical nation of Israel, engineered and supported by virtually all of World Jewry. The second beast is the great sponsor, backer, protector, defender, guard and enforcer for the first beast.

This second beast is undoubtedly the United States, which is today Zionist occupied territory. The leader of the United States, its President, is currently and has since the dawn of the 20th century, been a tool and stooge of powerful Zionist forces within and without its borders. There have been two notable exceptions—President John F. Kennedy and Richard M. Nixon—and these two were harshly dealt with as punishment for their courageous but futile resistance to the reigning parasitic host, the Zionist Jews.

The 50 states of the United States are often described as having been carved out of the North American wilderness. The ancient nation of Israel, the Old Testament records, having escaped Pharaoic Egyptian captivity, wandered in the wilderness until finally the people reached the "Promised Land." For many immigrants to the United States, it, too, was and is envisioned as the "Promised Land." Are these further signs and indications of the common destiny of these two pro-Zionist powers, the United States and Israel?

Revelation 13 tells us that the number of the beast that comes up out of the earth is 666 and that this is the number of a man. But do not confuse the beast and the man. Though they are two different entities, the two are allied in that the man and the beast both have the same identifying occult number 666. It is therefore, the "number of the beast" and also the "number of a man" *(Revelation 13:18)*.

The second beast is a global power, a nation, or international group of allied nations (United Nations, Trilateral Commission, G20, etc.) and the man is the leader of this allied global system. By the weight of the evidence I present here, the nation that is pre-eminent in this international alliance, or grouping of world powers, is the United States of America.

So, to sum up, we have the first beast, satanic, physical Israel (and World Jewry, its backbone and money machine). The second beast, its sponsor, protector, and Praetorian guard attack dog and enforcer, is the United States and its globalist allies, and this great superpower nation is destined to be led by the man whose dreadful and revealing number is the same as that of the beast, 666.

The Awesome Power of the Two Beasts

Each of these beasts has great powers. The first beast, World Jewry, has the money power, including control of banking and natural resources (oil, precious metals), and also has potent spiritual power endowed to it by Satan. Thus, much of the Christian establishment has been usurped through World Jewry's Zionist propaganda and has been swallowed up by the floodwaters of the Lie.

Meanwhile, the second beast, the United States and its allies, has unique military capability and the complementary political, intelligence, and diplomatic potential that accompanies it. With its combined political and military brute force, the beast is the Global Policeman and enforcer of the New World Order.

What is significant is that the tremendous force of this second beast is applied toward achieving the objectives of the first beast, which is ultimately total global control.

The Holy Bible explains to us this occult mission and role of the second beast. Let us see what the Scriptures say:

> *"And he (the second beast, out of the earth) exerciseth all the power of the first beast before him, and causeth the earth and them which dwell therein to worship the first beast (out of the sea) whose deadly wound was healed."*
>
> —*Revelation 13:12*

The second beast is the United States and its global leader, the antichrist, the man with the beast's number 666. This second beast and its antichrist leader "exerciseth" all the power of the first beast, World Jewry, and thus has the money power at its disposal. With this money power and its own brute military muscle and diplomatic skills it causes the whole world to "worship"

World Jewry (Israel and the Jews), is the first beast, whose deadly wound was healed when Israel was re-established as a nation in 1948.

What we have here is an alliance of two great powers, the

first being Israel and World Jewry with its money and religious power, and the second being the United States with its political and military prowess.

The Whole World Marvels

This dual-beast unity and combination makes for what appears to be an unbeatable force, such that the whole world marvels and "worships" the beast, asking *"Who is like unto the beast? Who is able to make war with him?"*

The prophet Daniel prophesied that the final kingdom that would envelop the globe would be one whose leader would not worship the God of his fathers, but, in his place worship instead a *"God of Forces."*

> *"And the king shall do according to his will; and he shall exalt himself, and magnify himself above every god, and shall speak marvellous things against the God of gods, and shall prosper till the indignation be accomplished: for that that is determined shall be done.*
>
> *"Neither shall he regard the God of his fathers, nor the desire of women, nor regard any god: for he shall magnify himself above all.*
>
> *"But in his estate shall he honour the God of Forces: and a god whom his fathers knew not shall he honour with gold, and silver, and with precious stones, and pleasant things.*
>
> *"Thus shall he do in the most strong holds with a strange god, whom he shall acknowledge and increase with glory: and he shall cause them to rule*

over many, and shall divide the land for gain."
—Daniel 11:36-39

A Jewish Kingdom: the U.S.A. and World Jewry Together

We see confirmed in *Daniel* the prophecies of *Revelation 13*, in which the great endtime kingdom that conquers and devours the whole earth will be *Jewish*, for its king will worship a "god whom his fathers knew not." Instead he will honor a strange god, with "gold, and silver, and with precious stones, and pleasant things."

His fathers—Abraham, Moses, Isaac, Jacob, Jeremiah, Isaiah, David and other heroes of ancient Israel once worshipped the true God of heaven, but the last days king of Israel will worship a God of Forces, a militaristic, world-conquering deity. And he will honor this strange god with money and gold. Thus we see once again a combination of military and money power, just as is true of today's U.S.A.-Israel dual kingdom.

The Kabbalah introduces to the world an entire complex of gods and goddesses, chief of which is the Holy Serpent, Leviathan, Leviathan is, indeed, a "strange god," the God of Forces.

Daniel goes on to say that this last days king will *"enter also into the glorious land and many countries will be overthrown" (Daniel 11:41)*. He shall also *"have power over the treasuries of gold, and of silver, and over all the precious things of Egypt, and the Libyans and the Ethiopians..." (Daniel 11:43)*.

"Therefore he shall go forth with great fury to destroy, and utterly to make away many," and "he shall plant the tabernacles of his palace between the seas in the glorious holy mountain..." (Daniel 11:44-45).

Today, the United States and World Jewry (including the

country of Israel) do, indeed, have power over the treasures of gold, silver, and all precious things. Giant banks such as JP Morgan Chase, Bank of America, Morgan Stanley, U.S. Bank, Wells Fargo, Morgan Stanley, and Goldman Sachs control and manipulate the precious metals and commodities markets. The countries of Egypt, Libya, and Ethiopia have been brought into America's and World Jewry's orbit, and the oil and minerals of Africa and the Middle East are in the grasp of this Zionist duo.

In 1948, only with the diplomatic approval of the United States was Israel able to achieve U.N recognition and nation-status, making possible the fulfillment of the endtime prophecy that the coming king, the antichrist, "shall plant the tabernacles of his palace between the seas, in the glorious holy mountain" (i.e. in Jerusalem—see *Daniel 9:16*).

Now this last days king, *Daniel* instructs us, *"shall work deceitfully"* and *"shall become strong with a small people" (Daniel 11:23)*. This is most definitely a picture of Israel and the Jews working deceitfully to acquire a kingdom for themselves. Their strength is manifested in spite of the fact that the Jews are numerically "a small people."

Daniel further says that this king (the antichrist) will conquer and have dominion over "the fattest places of the province" and he shall do that *"which his fathers have not done, nor his fathers' fathers."* Indeed with America's military tie to Israel, every nation which the Jews have locked horns with has gone down to defeat, including Palestine, Egypt, Lebanon, Iraq, and Afghanistan.

The Beasts of Revelation Make War Against the Saints of God

The final foe of Satan's beast powers will be the "holy people," Christians who know the true god:

> *"...When he shall have accomplished to scatter the power of the holy people, all these things (prophetic events) shall be finished."*
>
> *—Daniel 12:7*

This prophecy in *Daniel* confirms that the prophecy found in *Revelation 13*, in which the beast *"makes war against the saints and overcomes them."* Yet, he himself will eventually suffer a resounding defeat as Christ comes and puts an end to the vain-glory desire of Satan, his antichrist, and the forces allied against God and His people.

The kingdom of this latter days king will, says Daniel, be a *beast* kingdom, *"which shall be diverse from all kingdoms, and shall devour the whole earth and shall tread it down, and break it in pieces."* Its wicked ruler, the antichrist, possessed by Leviathan the Serpent, will reign over an expansive domain.

In every respect the beast of *Daniel* that devours the whole world *"in the latter days"* and wages war against the saints of God is like unto the second beast described in *Revelation 13*. This beast that comes up out of the earth is the one that causes the whole world to worship and honor Israel and World Jewry. Through his satanic power and miracles he elevates the Jews to the pinnacle of world power. Like *Daniel's* beast, the second beast of *Revelation 13* deceives the masses and causes all the world "to receive a mark in their right hand or forehead." No person can buy or sell unless he has this "mark, or the name of the beast, or the number of his name" *(Revelation 13:17).*

The Battle of Armageddon

Both Daniel, and John, in *Revelation 13*, remark that this wicked, last days beast does not cease his blaspheming against Christ and his war against the saints of God. Working with the power of Satan and of unclean spirits which are the *"spirits of devils"* the kings of the earth are gathered to battle in a place called *"Armageddon" (Revelation 16:12-16)*.

Armageddon is a desolate physical place in Israel formally called the "Valley of Megiddo." Bible prophecy points to this location in the Middle East as the site of a lethal endtime battle. It is clear from current history that military and political forces are converging on this geographical site. Nuclear-armed Israel continues to receive high-tech military weapons from the United States and from Britain, France, and Germany. Indeed, military experts rank tiny Israel, amply supplied with the most advanced military weapons and equipment by its ally, the United States, among the world's premier military powers.

Meanwhile, the United States marauds in this Middle East region with hundreds of thousands of young Americans fighting (and dying) in countries like Iraq, Afghanistan, and Pakistan. The U.S.-Israeli juggernaut now threatens to invade Yemen, Syria, and Iran, among others. The immediate goal of this U.S.-Israeli coalition is two fold: The acquisition of the Middle East's huge store of oil and the setting up of a "Greater Israel" to reign and rule over the defeated Arab and Persian peoples. The ultimate goal is the conquest of the world and the establishment of the Jewish Utopia.

God's Prophetic Word A Wonder to Behold

This, then, is the chronicle of the two beasts of Bible prophecy, which the Kabbalah says are the two beasts that comprise the two Leviathan serpents, one from up out of the abyss of the bottomless pit (the sea of chaos); the second from the wilderness; that is up out of the earth.

The Bible's book of *Revelation* has even more to say

about these two beasts. In *Revelation 17* we are instructed regarding the spiritual and religious system described as *"Mystery Babylon, the Mother of harlots and abominations."* This fabulously wicked "Mother of harlots and abominations" is seen to be riding a great beast that devours the whole world. Is not this a description of the same two, endtime beasts described in *Revelation 13* and in *Daniel*?

The magnificent manner in which God's prophetic word is clarified and re-emphasized is often a wonder to behold. In *Deuteronomy 31:29* we find this prophecy, uttered by Moses just prior to his passing away and going to be with the Lord. He prophesied to the ultimate destiny of the House of Israel, saying:

> *"...and evil will befall you in the latter days; because ye will do evil in the sight of the Lord, to provoke him to anger through the work of your hands."*

It is of a truth that man and Satan make plans and hatch plots. But God decides and judges all things. He has already judged the evil plans of the rabbis for a great Feast of the Beast: *"...and evil will befall you in the latter days," says God's Word.*

SIX

The Fall of Leviathan and the Victory of Christ Jesus

"For Moses truly said unto the fathers, A prophet shall the Lord your God raise up unto you…Ye are the children of the prophets, and of the covenant which god made with our fathers, saying unto Abraham, And in thy seed shall all the kindreds of the earth be blessed. Unto you first God, having raised up his Son, Jesus sent Him to bless you…"

—*Acts 3:22-26*

In the above scripture, we find that Moses prophesied to Israel of the "prophet" that God would raise up. Abraham likewise was told that this prophet sent by God will bless all the kindreds (nations and peoples) on earth. *This prophet is the very Son of God, Jesus.*

In *Acts 4:8-12* we find confirmation that Jesus is the blessing sent to Israel and to the whole world by God:

"Then Peter, filled with the Holy Ghost, said unto them, Ye rulers of the people, and elders of Israel...

"Be it known unto you all, and to all the people of Israel, that by the name of Jesus Christ of Nazareth, whom ye crucified, whom God raised from the dead...

"This is the Stone which was set at nought of you builders, which is become head of the corner.

"Neither is there salvation in any other: for there is none other name whereby we must be saved."

He Has Given Us the New Covenant

Repentance is thus come to the Jews and to all of humanity in the person of Jesus Christ. Replacing the Old, He has given us the New Covenant. All who believe in Christ by faith join in this New Covenant. They are blessed by it, and its precepts are written on their hearts.

The Scriptures tell us that "as many of you who have been baptized into Christ have put on Christ" *(Galatians 3: 27)*:

"There is neither Jew nor Greek, there is neither bond nor free, there is neither male nor female: for ye are one in Christ Jesus.

And if ye be Christ's, then are ye Abraham's seed, and heirs according to the promise."

—Galatians 3:28-29

You Must Choose

The Jew, no different than the Gentile, must choose between God and Leviathan. Will you believe in Christ Jesus, or will you accept what your rabbis tell you about Leviathan, the Serpent?

In the Jews' religion, the rabbis proclaim, there is coming a *Great Day of Purification*. It will, they say be a time of joy, glory and exaltation for Jews, but also a time of great agony and misery for the Gentiles who reject Leviathan as "Messiah."

The rabbis are wrong. Terribly wrong. The Scriptures make plain that the Serpent is doomed to external torment in hell. And all who are seduced by his wiles and enchanted by his lies will join him. His Great Day of Purification will end in abject failure. We read in the Scriptures, in *Isaiah 27:1*, of the tragic end of the Serpent Leviathan:

> *"In that day the LORD with his sore and great and strong sword shall punish leviathan the piercing serpent, even leviathan that crooked serpent; and he shall slay the dragon that is in the sea."*

My plea is that you turn from fables and lies to the eternal truth that is Jesus Christ. By faith, Jesus will take you in and forever cherish and hold you in his arms. Only believe.

> *"As it is written, Behold, I lay in Sion a stumblingstone and rock of offence: and whosoever believeth on him shall not be ashamed."*
>
> *—Romans 9:33*

ABOUT THE AUTHOR

Well-known author of the #1 national bestseller, *Dark Secrets of The New Age*, Texe Marrs has written books for such major publishers as Simon & Schuster, John Wiley, Prentice Hall/Arco, McGraw-Hill, and Dow Jones-Irwin. His books have sold millions of copies. He is one of the world's foremost symbologists and is a first-rate scholar of ancient history and Mystery religions.

Texe Marrs was assistant professor of aerospace studies, teaching American defense policy, strategic weapons systems, and related subjects at the University of Texas at Austin for five years. He has also taught international affairs, political science, and psychology for two other universities. A graduate *summa cum laude* from Park College, Kansas City, Missouri, he earned his Master's degree at North Carolina State University.

As a career USAF officer (now retired), he commanded communications-electronics and engineering units. He holds a number of military decorations including the Vietnam Service Medal and Presidential Unit Citation, and has served in Germany, Italy, and throughout Asia.

President of *RiverCrest Publishing* in Austin, Texas, Texe Marrs is a frequent guest on radio and TV talk shows throughout the U.S.A. and Canada. His monthly newsletter, *Power of Prophecy*, is distributed around the world, and he is heard globally on his popular, international shortwave and internet radio program, *Power of Prophecy*. His articles and research are published regularly on his exclusive website: *powerofprophecy.com*.

FOR OUR NEWSLETTER

Texe Marrs offers a free sample copy of his newsletter focusing on world events, false religion, and secret societies, cults, and the occult challenge to Christianity. If you would like to receive this newsletter, please write to:

Power of Prophecy
1708 Patterson Road
Austin, Texas 78733

You may also e-mail your request to:
customerservice1@powerofprophecy.com

FOR OUR WEBSITE

Texe Marrs' newsletter is published free monthly on our website. This website has descriptions of all Texe Marrs' books, and are packed with interesting, insight-filled articles, videos, breaking news, and other information. You also have the opportunity to order an exciting array of books, tapes, and videos through our online Catalog and Sales Store. Visit our website at:

www.powerofprophecy.com

OUR SHORTWAVE RADIO PROGRAM

Texe Marrs' international radio program, *Power of Prophecy*, is broadcast weekly on shortwave radio throughout the United States and the world. *Power of Prophecy* can be heard on WWCR at 4.840 on Sunday nights at 9:00 p.m. Central Time. You may also listen to *Power of Prophecy* 24/7 on website *powerofprophecy.com.*

MORE RESOURCES FOR YOU

Books:

(For all orders, please include shipping and handling charge)

The Destroyer—The Antichrist is at Hand, by Texe Marrs (192 pages) $20

Holy Serpent of the Jews—The Rabbis' Secret Plan for Satan to Crush Their Enemies and Vault the Jews to Global Dominion, by Texe Marrs (224 pages) $20

DNA Science and the Jewish Bloodline, by Texe Marrs (256 pages) $20

Bloody Zion—Refuting the Jewish Fables That Sustain Israel's War Against God and Man, by Edward Hendrie (544 pages) $28

Conspiracy of the Six-Pointed Star—Eye Opening Revelations and Forbidden Knowledge About Israel, the Jews, Zionism, and the Rothschilds, by Texe Marrs (432 pages) $25

Codex Magica—Secret Signs, Mysterious Symbols, and Hidden Codes of the Illuminati, by Texe Marrs (624 pages) $35

Judaism's Strange Gods, by Michael Hoffman (381 pages) $22

Matrix of Gog—From the Land of Magog Came the Khazars to Destroy and Plunder, by Daniel Patrick (160 pages) $18

On the Jews and Their Lies, by Martin Luther (240 pages) $20

Protocols of the Learned Elders of Zion (320 Pages) $20

Solving the Mystery of Babylon the Great, by Edward Hendrie (388 pages) $25

Videos:

Cauldron of Abaddon—"From Jerusalem and Israel Flow a Torrent of Satanic Evil and Mischief Endangering the Whole World" (DVD) $25

Illuminati Mystery Babylon—The Hidden Elite of Israel, America, and Russia, and Their Quest for Global Dominion (DVD) $25

Marching to Zion (DVD) $20

Masonic Lodge Over Jerusalem—The Hidden Rulers of Israel, the Coming World War in the Middle East and the Rebuilding of the Temple (DVD) $25

Thunder Over Zion—Illuminati Bloodlines and the Secret Plan for A Jewish Utopia and a New World Messiah (DVD) $25

Please add 10% for shipping in the United States (minimum $5)
Texas residents add taxes of 6.75%
International Shipping: Please add 70% (minimum $30)

Order Now! Use your MasterCard, Visa,
Discover, or American Express
You may order from our website: www.powerofprophecy.com
Or you may phone 1-800-234-9673,
or send check or money order to:
Power of Prophecy 1708 Patterson Road, Austin, Texas 78733

Check Out This Web Site for more invaluable
books, videos, audiotapes, and for breaking news and informative articles: www.powerofprophecy.com